From Our Home To Yours

Homestead Vegetables

RHUBARB

Ann Edall-Robson

Title: From Our Home To Yours: Homestead Vegetables - Rhubarb
Author: Ann Edall-Robson

Publisher: 1449511 Alberta Ltd.
P.O. Box 10181
Airdrie, Alberta, Canada
T4A 0H5

Copyright @ 2019 by Ann Edall-Robson
First Edition - 2019

All rights reserved. No part of this publication may be reproduced in any form, or by any means, electronic or mechanical, including photocopying, recording, or any information browsing, storage, or retrieval systems, without permission in writing from the publisher.

The author and the publisher have made every effort to ensure the information in this book is accurate.

Cover Photo by Ann Edall-Robson (DAKATAMA™)
Interior Illustrations by Alesha Buczny

ISBN
(Hardcover) 978-0-9959787-8-2
(Paperback) 978-0-9959787-7-5
(E-Book) 978-0-9959787-9-9

Homestead Vegetables - Rhubarb

Homestead Vegetables - Rhubarb

"Hon, I'm sure somebody will like the taste of that recipe."

Steven W. West

Homestead Vegetables - Rhubarb

INDEX

BEVERAGES

Julep	1
Liqueur	2
Mint Cocktail	3
Rum Slush	4
Stock	5
Wine	6

CAKES, COOKIES, MUFFINS & SQUARES

Buttermilk Coffee Cake	9
Cream Cheese Rhubarb Brownies	11
Crunch Cake	13
Matrimonial Bars	15
Oatmeal Cookies	17
Norwegian Rhubarb Cake	19
Pudding Cake	21
Rhubarb Custard Cake	22
Simple Up-Side-Down Cake	23
Sour Cream Cookies	24
Sour Cream Muffins	26
Sour Milk Cake	27

CANDY

Buttons and Strings	31
Coconut Strawberry Popsicles	33
Dip Sticks	34
Gummy Treats	35
Leather	37

DESSERTS

Charlotte	41
Cheesecake	42
Honey Snake Fence	44
Sweet Rolls	46
Tapioca Pudding	48

HOME PRESERVES

Hints for Canning & Preserves	51
Apple Rhubarb Jam	52
Onion Rhubarb Relish	54
Pickling Rhubarb	55
Rhubarb Jelly	56
Rhubarb Marmalade	57
Salsa - Rhubarb Style	58
Saskatoon Rhubarb Jam	59
Strawberry Rhubarb Compote	60
Strawberry Rhubarb Jam	62

PIE

Dandelion Rhubarb Pie	65
Custard Rhubarb Pie	66
Humble Rhubarb Pie	67
Old Fashioned Rhubarb Pie	68
Rhubarb Meringue Pie	69
Sour Cream Rhubarb Pie	71
Strawberry Rhubarb Pie	73

EXTRA RECIPES, HINTS & MEASUREMENT CONVERSIONS

Kitchen Hints	77
Equivalent Charts	79
Buttery Liqueur Sauce	80
Crumble Topping	81
Homestyle Vanilla	82
Old Fashioned Matrimonial Cake	83
Pie Pastry	85
Rhubarb Vinaigrette	86
Sour Milk	87
Gardening with Rhubarb	89
Notes From The Author	93
Books by the Author	94
Reference	95

All of recipes in this book use fresh rhubarb, unless otherwise noted.
All of the recipes in this book use all-purpose flour, butter, granulated white sugar, unless otherwise noted.
The Extras section, and Helpful Hints section, offer additional recipes and suggestions to enhance cooking with From Our Home To Yours cookbooks.

Homestead Vegetables - Rhubarb

Homestead Vegetables - Rhubarb

BEVERAGES

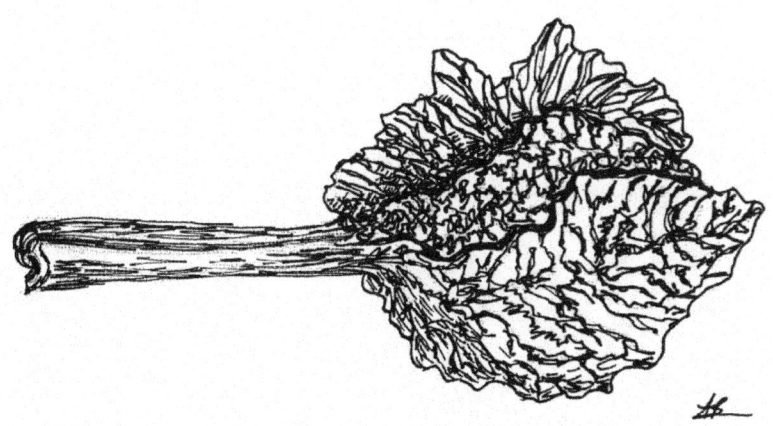

Julep

Ingredients

Syrup

2 cups	Rhubarb Stock	500 mL
3/4 cup	Sugar	175 mL

Directions

Syrup - Place rhubarb stock and sugar in a medium sized saucepan. Cook over medium heat until sugar is dissolved. Stir occasionally. Increase heat to medium high and bring the syrup to a boil. Boil for one minute. Remove from heat. Cool.

To Serve - All Julep beverages start with 1/4 cup (60 mL) of syrup.

Pour syrup into a highball glass, add crushed ice, 1 ounce (60 mL) of bourbon, and a splash of water. Garnish with a mint sprig and a rhubarb stir stick.

Pour syrup into a tall glass, add crushed ice and carbonated beverage of choice. Garnish with a mint sprig and a rhubarb stir stick.

Suggestions

Notes

Liqueur

Ingredients

6 tablespoons	Sugar	90 mL
1/4 cup	Water	60 mL
3 1/2 cups	Fresh Rhubarb	875 mL
3 cups	Vodka	750 mL
1/2 cup	Grand Marnier	125 mL

One large, sealable, jar. Big enough to hold all of the ingredients.

Directions

In a small saucepan, add sugar and water. Bring to a boil. Continue to boil until the sugar dissolves. Remove from heat. Cool.

Coarsely chop rhubarb into 1/2" (1.27 cm) pieces and place in a sealable jar.

Mix Vodka, Grand Marnier, and sugar water together. Pour over rhubarb. Stir.

Tightly seal the jar and leave at room temperature for three weeks. The rhubarb should have no colour left and the liqueur will have taken on the colour of the rhubarb.

Strain the mixture through a sieve. Discard rhubarb.

Bottle in individual, smaller jars.

Suggestions

Drink as is, or top with ginger-ale, tonic water, sparkling water, or sprite.

Notes

Mint Cocktail

Ingredients

1	Orange	1
2	Lemons	2
4 cups	Fresh Rhubarb	1 L
2 cups	Water	500 mL
1 teaspoon	Orange Zest	5 mL
2 teaspoons	Lemon Zest	10 mL
1 1/2 cups	Sugar	375 mL
1 cup	Hot Water	250 mL
5 - 10	Fresh Mint Leaves	5 - 10

Directions

Squeeze juice from the orange and lemons. Set aside.

Grate the rind (zest) from the orange and lemons. Set aside.

Chop rhubarb into 1/2" (1.27 cm) pieces.

Simmer rhubarb, water, and zests together until rhubarb is soft. Strain through a sieve or piece of cheesecloth. Discard rhubarb.

Place sugar and hot water in a small saucepan. Simmer until sugar has dissolved. Remove from heat and cool for 10 minutes before adding to rhubarb juice. Add orange and lemon juice.

Place mint leaves in a pitcher, add rhubarb juice mixture, and refrigerate for several hours, until the desired flavour of mint is reached.

Suggestions

Serve over crushed ice. Garnish with slices of orange, lemon and a mint leaf.

Notes

Rum Slush

Ingredients

1 cup	Very Strong Tea - Cooled	250 mL
10 cups	Fresh Rhubarb	2.5 L
7 cups	Water	1.75 L
2 cups	Sugar	500 mL
1-12 oz. can	Frozen Orange Juice	355 mL
1-12 oz. can	Frozen Lemonade Juice	355 mL
3 cups	White Rum	750 mL

Directions

Make a pot of regular tea. Leave the bag in the pot to steep as it cools.

Mix sugar and water in a large saucepan. Bring to a boil.

Chop rhubarb into 1/2" (1.27 cm) pieces.

Place rhubarb in a large saucepan. Cover with water. No more than 1" (2.54 cm) above the rhubarb. Boil until rhubarb is soft. Remove from the heat. Cool.

Mix rhubarb with sugar water, tea, juices, and rum. Place in one-gallon (3.8 L) ice cream pails (use 2) or equivalent sized containers with lids. Freeze.

Suggestions

To serve, place 3/4 cup (175 mL) of slush in a glass and top with with your choice of ginger ale, tonic water, sparkling water, or sprite.

Notes

Stock

Ingredients

2 cups	Rhubarb	500 mL
4 cups	Water	1 L

Directions

Chop rhubarb into 1/2" (1.27cm) pieces. Use fresh or frozen rhubarb.

Place the rhubarb and water together in a medium-sized saucepan. Bring to a boil. Reduce heat and simmer for at least 30 minutes. Remove from heat. Cool

Strain the rhubarb from the juice. Discard rhubarb pulp.

Makes approximately 2 cups (500 mL).

Store in sealed jars in a cool place or unsealed in the fridge for 2-3 weeks.

Suggestions

Rhubarb Stock is used in quite a few of the recipes in this book, Gummy Treats and Rhubarb Jelly to name a few.

Pour 1/3 cup (75 mL) over ice and fill the glass with water, tonic water or club soda.

Notes

Wine

Ingredients

10 pounds	Rhubarb	4.5 Kg
2 gallons	Cold Water	8 L
3 1/2 - 3 3/4 pounds	Sugar	1.6 to 1.7 Kg
1	Orange rind	1
1	Lemon rind	1
1/2 oz	Fresh Ginger Root	15 mL
1/4 oz	Isinglass (A kind of gelatin found in a thin transparent sheet)	7.5 mL
1/4 cup	Warm Water	60 mL

Directions

Wash rhubarb; cut into 1" (2.54 cm) pieces and place in a large crockery pot. Add cold water, cover with crockery pot lid and leave for five days. After this time, strain the liquid off through a sieve or cheesecloth. Press the liquid out of the pulp. Do not allow any pulp to pass through. Discard pulp.

Measure liquid; allow 3 1/2 to 3 3/4 pounds (1.6 to 1.7 Kg) of sugar to each gallon (3.8 L). The amount will be dependent on the acidity of the mixture.

Stir well, re-cover and leave for another five days, stirring twice daily.

On day ten, pour the liquid into a clean cask. Peel orange and lemon and slice peel into fine strips. Peel ginger root and slice thinly. Dissolve the isinglass in warm water. Add isinglass, root ginger, and the orange and lemon rinds to the rhubarb mixture. Cover the cask bung hole tightly with a cloth.

When liquid ceases to work or bubble, remove the ginger, lemon, and orange rind. Either bung the cask securely or pour off the wine and bottle it.

Let age for 6 to 12 months before using.

Suggestions

Notes

Homestead Vegetables - Rhubarb

CAKES

COOKIES

MUFFINS

SQUARES

Buttermilk Coffee Cake

Ingredients

Cake

1 1/2 - 3 cups	Fresh Rhubarb	375 - 750 mL
1/2 cup	Butter	125 mL
1 1/2 cups	Brown Sugar	625 mL
1	Egg	1
1 cup	Buttermilk	250 mL
1 teaspoon	Baking Soda	5 mL
1/2 teaspoon	Salt	2.5 mL
2 cups	Flour	500 mL

Topping

1/4 cup	Brown Sugar	60 mL
1 1/2 teaspoons	Ground Cinnamon	7.5 mL
1/4 cup	Chopped Nuts - See Suggestions	60 mL

Directions

Preheat oven to 350 F (175 C).

Grease a 9" x 13" (22 x 33 cm) cake pan.

Chop rhubarb into 1/4" (.635 cm) pieces.

Topping - In a small bowl, mix brown sugar, cinnamon and nuts together. Set aside.

Cake - In a small bowl, whisk together the flour, baking soda and salt. Set aside.

Dredge the rhubarb with one tablespoon (15 mL) of the flour mixture. Set aside.

Cream together butter and brown sugar. Add egg and mix until blended.

Add dry ingredients alternately with buttermilk. Mix until well blended. Fold in the rhubarb.

Pour batter into the prepared cake pan and sprinkle topping evenly over the top.

Bake for 35 to 40 minutes, or until a toothpick comes out clean.

Suggestions

The quantity of the rhubarb used depends entirely on your taste.

Our original recipe calls for walnuts to be used in the topping. Use almonds, cashews, and pecans as an alternative.

Notes

Cream Cheese Rhubarb Brownies

Brownies, cream cheese, and rhubarb make for a sweet-savoury combination.

Ingredients

1 cup	Fresh Rhubarb	250 mL
1 cup	Semi-Sweet Chocolate Chips	250 mL
1/2 cup	Butter	125 mL
1/4 cup	Sugar	60 mL
1 cup	Cream Cheese - Not the Soft/Spreadable Kind	1 - 250g Pkg
2 tablespoons	Sugar	30 mL
1	Egg Yolk	1
1/2 teaspoon	Cornstarch	2.5 mL
2	Large Eggs	2
1 cup	Flour	250 mL
1 good pinch	Salt	1 good pinch
1 cup	Sugar	250 mL
1 teaspoon	Vanilla	5 mL

Directions

Preheat oven to 350 F (175 C).

Line an 8" x 8" (20 x 20 cm) or 9" x 9" (22 x 22 cm) pan with parchment paper.

Cut rhubarb into 1/2" (1.27cm) pieces.

Melt chocolate chips and butter in a small pan. Stir to blend. Remove from heat and cool for about 20 minutes. Mixture must be cool. This is a must, or the eggs will cook and separate versus blend when added to the chocolate mixture.

Cook rhubarb and 1/4 cup (60 mL) of sugar together over medium heat until the rhubarb is soft. Continue cooking until mixture reduces and is thick. Remove from heat and set aside to cool—strain off any liquid.

Beat together cream cheese and 2 tablespoons (30 mL) of sugar until smooth.

Blend in egg yolk, add cornstarch, and continue beating until it is well blended.

Beat two eggs in a small dish.

Blend 1 cup (250 mL) of flour and salt together.

Add 1 cup (250 mL) of sugar and vanilla to the melted and cooled chocolate. Beat until smooth. Slowly add the beaten eggs. Mix well until it has a smooth and glossy texture. Add flour mixture 1/4 cup at a time. Mix well after each addition.

Pour chocolate mixture into the pan. Spread evenly.

Add alternating dollops of cream cheese mixture and rhubarb to the top of the chocolate mixture. Use the back of a spoon or a butter knife to swirl together.

Bake for 50 minutes or until a toothpick comes out clean.

Suggestions

Use a slotted spoon to add rhubarb to top of chocolate mixture. This will help to remove excess liquid.

Notes

Crunch Cake

An excellent cake to take to a potluck.

Ingredients

Cake

3 1/2 cups	Fresh Rhubarb	875 mL
1-3oz. box	Strawberry Jello	85 g
2 cups	Flour	500 mL
1 teaspoon	Baking Powder	5 mL
1/2 teaspoon	Baking Soda	2.5 mL
1/2 teaspoon	Salt	2.5 mL
1 cup	Butter	250 mL
1 1/4 cup	Sugar	310 mL
2	Eggs	2
1 cup	Sour Cream	250 mL

Topping

1/2 cup	Brown Sugar	125 mL
2 teaspoons	White Vinegar	10 mL
1 teaspoon	Cinnamon	5 mL
1/2 cup	Chopped Nuts	125 mL

Directions

Preheat oven to 350 F (175 C).

Grease a 9" x 13" (22 x 33 cm) cake pan.

Cut rhubarb into 1/4" to 1/2" (.635 to 1.27 cm) pieces. Sprinkle Jello powder over rhubarb. Mix to coat. Set aside.

Topping - In a small bowl, mix brown sugar, vinegar, cinnamon, and nuts together. Set aside.

Cake - In a small bowl, whisk together flour, baking powder, baking soda and salt. Set aside.
Beat butter and sugar together until smooth. Add eggs one at a time, just until blended. Add flour mixture and sour cream alternately, ending with the sour cream.

Spread half of the batter into the cake pan. Sprinkle half the topping mixture evenly over the batter. Add the remaining batter. Finish with topping.

Bake for 45 to 50 minutes or until a toothpick inserted in the centre comes out clean.

Serve warm with ice-cream or whipped cream.

Suggestions

The original recipe calls for walnuts. We have used almonds, cashews, pecans and pistachio.

Double the Topping recipe for added texture and flavour.

Notes

Matrimonial Bars

The rich goodness of date-filled Matrimonial Bars takes a backseat to their rhubarb-filled cousin.

Ingredients

Filling

4 cups	Rhubarb	1 L
1 1/2 cups	Sugar	625 mL
2 tablespoon	Cornstarch	30 mL
1 teaspoon	Vanilla	5 mL
1 teaspoon	Lemon or Orange Zest	5 mL

Crust

1 1/2 cups	Oats - Quick Cook	625 mL
1 1/2 cups	Flour	625 mL
1/2 teaspoon	Baking Soda	2.5 mL
1 teaspoon	Baking Powder	5 mL
1 pinch	Salt	1 pinch
1 cup	Brown Sugar	250 mL
1 cup	Butter	250 mL

Directions

Preheat oven to 350 F (175 C).

Cut rhubarb into 1/4" (.635 cm) pieces.

Filling - Combine the rhubarb, sugar, cornstarch, vanilla, and zest in a saucepan. Cook slowly over a medium heat until thick. Cool completely.

Crust - In a bowl, blend oats, flour, baking soda, baking powder, salt, and brown sugar together. Cube butter and add to oat mixture. Blend by hand or with a pastry cutter until crumbly.
Press 2/3 of the mixture into a greased 9" x 9" (22 x 22 cm) baking pan. Add the cooled filling, then sprinkle with remaining oat mixture and bake for 30 to 35 minutes. Cool completely before cutting.
Freezes well.

Suggestions

Double the crust part of the recipe and make a batch of date-filled bars. See Old Fashioned Matrimonial Bars recipe in the Extras section.

Notes

Oatmeal Cookies

Oatmeal cookies are versatile. Adding rhubarb to them is one of the many extras you can include.

Ingredients

1 1/2 cups	Fresh Rhubarb	375 mL
3/4 cup + 1 1/2 tablespoons	Flour	175 mL + 22 mL
1/2 teaspoon	Baking Soda	2.5 mL
1/2 teaspoon	Ground Cinnamon	2.5 mL
1/4 teaspoon	Nutmeg	1 mL
1/2 teaspoon	Salt	2.5 mL
1/4 cup + 1 1/2 teaspoons	Nuts (Optional)	67.5 mL
1/2 cup	Chocolate Chips	125 mL
1/4 cup	Butter - Softened	60 mL
1/4 cup	Sugar	60 mL
1/4 cup + 1 1/2 tablespoons	Brown Sugar - Firm Packed	67.5 mL
1	Egg	1
3/4 teaspoon	Vanilla	3.5 mL
1 1/2 cups	Oats - Quick Cook	375 mL

Directions

Preheat oven to 375 F (190 C).

Line cookie sheets with parchment paper.

In a bowl, blend flour, baking soda, cinnamon, nutmeg, and salt together. Set aside.

Cut rhubarb into 1/4" (.635 cm) pieces and dredge with one tablespoon (15 mL) of the flour mixture.

Finely chop the nuts. Add nuts and chocolate chips to rhubarb. Stir to coat. Set aside.

Beat butter, white, and brown sugar together until creamy. Add egg and vanilla. Blend. Add flour mixture. Mix well. Add oats and rhubarb mixture. Mix in with a wooden spoon.

Drop by large spoonful onto cookie sheets.

Bake for 9 - 12 minutes.

Remove from the oven and let stand for 1 minute before moving to a rack to cool completely.

Suggestions

For added flavour, use fresh grated nutmeg.

Change out chocolate chips with any type of flavoured chocolate chips, raisins, or craisins. Use your imagination.

To make soft cookies, remove them from the oven a minute or two early.

Recipe can easily be doubled and freezes well.

Notes

Norwegian Rhubarb Cake

Your heritage is a wonderful place to find recipes

Ingredients

Cake

3 1/2 cups	Fresh Rhubarb	875 mL
2 cups	Flour	500 mL
3 teaspoons	Baking Powder	15 mL
1/2 teaspoon	Salt	2.5 mL
1 cup	Butter - Softened	250 mL
1 cup	Sugar	250 mL
2/3 cup	Buttermilk	150 mL
3	Eggs	3
1 teaspoon	Vanilla	5 mL

Topping

2 tablespoons	Course Sugar	30 mL
1/4 teaspoon	Cinnamon	1 mL

Directions

Preheat oven to 350 F (175 C).

Grease a 9" or 10" (23 or 25 cm) round cake pan. Line the bottom with parchment paper to fit.

Blend together flour, baking powder, and salt. Set aside.

Cut rhubarb into 1/2" pieces (1.27 cm). Dredge with one tablespoon (15 mL) of the flour mixture. Set aside.

Cream the butter and sugar. Add buttermilk and mix. Add eggs, one at a time, mixing until each is well blended. Add the vanilla.

Slowly add the dry ingredients to the buttermilk mixture. Mix well.

Fold the rhubarb into the batter.

Pour mixture into the prepared pan and sprinkle first with sugar and then with cinnamon, if desired.

Bake for 45 - 60 minutes. At 45 minutes check doneness by inserting a toothpick in the centre. You want it to come out clean. If additional baking is needed, check centre at 5 minutes intervals until it is done to your liking. Remove from the oven and cool for at least 30 minutes before serving.

Serve warm or at room temperature, plain or with your choice of ice cream or whipped cream.

Suggestions

If using a springform pan, be sure to let the cake cool before loosening.

Notes

Pudding Cake

Not quite what you'd think a pudding would be, but it makes for a nice dessert at any time.

Ingredients

2 cups	Rhubarb	500 mL
1 3/4 cup	Sugar	425 mL
3 tablespoons	Butter - Softened	45 mL
1 teaspoon	Baking Powder	5 mL
1/4 teaspoon	Salt	1 mL
1 cup	Flour - Sifted	250 mL
1/2 cup	Milk	125 mL
1/2 teaspoon	Vanilla	2.5 mL
1/2 teaspoon	Almond Extract	2.5 mL
1 tablespoon	Cornstarch	15 mL
2/3 cup	Boiling Water	150 mL

Directions

Preheat oven to 375 F (190C).

Grease and flour a 9" x 9" (22 x 22 cm) cake pan.

Cut rhubarb into 1/4" (.635 cm) pieces. Dredge with one tablespoon (15 mL) of flour and spread evenly in the prepared cake pan.

Cream 3/4 cup (175 mL) of the sugar with butter.

Mix baking powder, salt, four together. Add vanilla and almond extract, milk. Blend with sugar mixture and pour over rhubarb. Mix remaining 1 cup (250 mL) of sugar and cornstarch together. Sprinkle over cake batter.

Slowly pour boiling water all over the batter. Do not mix. Bake for 45 minutes or until a toothpick inserted in the centre comes out clean.

Suggestions

Notes

Rhubarb Custard Cake

This is one of those quick and easy cakes that has lots of flavour and looks like you have been baking all day.

Ingredients

4 cups	Fresh Rhubarb	1 L
1 - 18 oz	Yellow Cake Mix	1 510g
1 teaspoon	Vanilla	5 mL
1 cup	Sugar	250 mL
1 cup	Whipping Cream	250 mL

Directions

Preheat oven to 350 F (175 C).

Cut rhubarb into 1/4" (.635 cm) pieces.

Prepare cake mix according to package instructions and pour into a 9" x 13" (22 x 33 cm) greased cake pan.

Sprinkle with rhubarb pieces.

Drizzle with vanilla.

Sprinkle sugar evenly over the surface of the cake mixture

Pour whipping cream, slowly, over the top

Bake for 40 to 45 minutes or until golden brown. Cool for 15 minutes before serving.

Suggestions

Store cake in the fridge.

Course sugar can be found in the cake decorating section at most grocery stores.

Notes

Simple Upside-Down Cake

I like to bake cakes from scratch, but I always keep one or two cake mixes in the pantry for back-up.

Ingredients

5 teaspoons	Butter	25 mL
2/3 cup	Brown Sugar	150 mL
4 cups	Rhubarb	1 L
1	White Cake Mix	1
	Ingredients listed on the package to mix into batter	

Directions

Preheat oven to 350 F (175 C).

Grease and flour a 10" x 6" x 2" (25 x 15 x 5 cm) cake pan or line it with parchment paper.

Cut rhubarb into 1/2" (1.27 cm) pieces.

Melt butter, remove from heat and stir in brown sugar. Spread over the bottom of the cake pan. Add rhubarb evenly over the bottom of the cake pan.

Prepare cake mix according to directions. Pour batter over rhubarb to within 1/2" (1.27 cm) to top of the pan.

Bake for 40 - 50 minutes or until cake is finished cooking. Remove from oven. Let it stand for 5 minutes.

To serve, place an inverted serving dish over the top of the cake pan. Turn the cooling pan over onto the serving dish. Remove the pan. Serve warm with whipped cream or ice cream.

Suggestions

Use any leftover cake batter to make cupcakes.

Notes

Sour Cream Cookies

Ingredients

2 cups	Fresh Rhubarb	500 mL
1 1/2 cups	Flour	625 mL
1 teaspoon	Baking Powder	5 mL
1/2 teaspoon	Baking Soda	2.5 mL
1/2 teaspoon	Salt	2.5 mL
1/2 cup	Butter - Softened	125 mL
3/4 cup	Sugar	175 mL
1	Egg	1
3/4 cup	Sour Cream	175 mL
1/2 teaspoon	Vanilla	2.5 mL

Directions

Preheat oven to 350 F (175 C).

Line cookie sheets with parchment paper.

In a bowl, blend flour, baking soda, baking powder, and salt together. Set aside.

Cut rhubarb into 1/4" (.635 cm) pieces. Dredge with one tablespoon (15 mL) of the flour mixture. Set aside.

Use an electric mixer, or by hand, beat butter and sugar together until light and fluffy. Add egg and mix until blended. Add sour cream and vanilla. Continue to blend until all ingredients are combined and have a smooth texture. Add flour mixture 1/4 cup (60 mL) at a time. Mix well after each addition. Fold rhubarb into the mixture. Mix by hand until incorporated.

Drop by large spoonful onto cookie sheets. Space about 2" (5 cm) apart as they will spread.

Bake for 10 - 12 minutes. The edges should be brown, and the tops should have a golden colour to them.

Remove from the oven and let stand for 1 minute before moving to a rack to cool completely.

Suggestions

Add 2/3 cup (150 mL) of chocolate chips or white chocolate chips.

Recipe can easily be doubled.

Notes

Sour Cream Muffins

Ingredients

1 1/2 cups	Fresh Rhubarb	375 mL
2 cups	Flour	500 mL
3/4 cup	Sugar	175 mL
2 1/2 teaspoons	Baking Powder	12.5 mL
1 teaspoon	Cinnamon	5 mL
1/2 teaspoon	Baking Soda	2.5 mL
1/2 teaspoon	Salt	2.5 mL
1 cup	Sour Cream	250 mL
1/2 cup	Butter - Melted	125 mL
2	Large Eggs	2
1 teaspoon	Vanilla	5 mL

Directions

Preheat oven to 400 F (200 C).

In a medium bowl, blend flour, sugar, baking powder, cinnamon, baking soda, and salt together. Set aside.

Cut rhubarb into 1/4" (.635 cm) pieces. Dredge with one tablespoon (15 mL) of the flour mixture. Set aside.

In a large bowl, mix together the sour cream and slightly cooled melted butter. Add eggs one at a time and mix until smooth and completely blended. Fold in sour cream mixture. Do not over mix.

Fold rhubarb into batter. Do not over mix. The dough should be heavy and thick.

Fill muffin tins almost full. If using muffin papers, fill to top edge. Bake for 18 - 22 minutes or until a toothpick inserted in the centre comes out clean. Remove from the oven. Let muffins sit for 1 minute before moving to a rack to cool.

Suggestions

Recipe can easily be doubled.

Notes

Sour Milk Cake

In times when refrigerators were a luxury, milk would be kept in the icehouse. If the milk went sour, it wasn't thrown out; it was used to bake with.

Ingredients

Cake

2 cups	Rhubarb	500 mL
2 cups	Four	500 mL
1 teaspoon	Baking Soda	5 mL
1 pinch	Salt	1 pinch
1/2 cup	Butter-Softened	125 mL
1 1/2 cups	Sugar	625 mL
1 teaspoon	Vanilla	5 mL
1	Egg	1
1 cup	Sour Milk	250 mL

Topping

1 cup	Brown Sugar	250 mL
1 teaspoon	Cinnamon	5 mL

Directions

Preheat oven to 350 F (175 C).

Grease a 9" x 13" (22 x 33 cm) cake pan.

Topping - In a small bowl, mix brown sugar and cinnamon. Set aside.

Cut rhubarb into 1/4" (.635 cm) pieces.

In a large bowl, combine flour, baking soda, and salt. Add rhubarb, and stir to coat all pieces with the flour mixture.

In a medium bowl, cream butter and sugar. Add vanilla, egg, and sour milk.

Fold wet ingredients into dry. Do not over mix.

Pour into the prepared cake pan, sprinkle with topping and bake for 35 minutes, or until a toothpick inserted in the centre comes out clean.

Suggestions

Notes

Homestead Vegetables - Rhubarb

Homestead Vegetables - Rhubarb

CANDY

Buttons and Strings

Ingredients

2 cups	Sugar	500 mL
1/2 cup	Water	125 mL
4	Fresh Rhubarb - Large Stalks	4

Directions

Syrup - Combine sugar and water in a large saucepan. Cook over medium heat until the sugar is dissolved. Remove from heat and allow it to cool.

Clean rhubarb.

Buttons
Slice stalks diagonally into 1/8" (.3175 cm) buttons.

Strings
Cut rhubarb stalks into 6" (15.24 cm) pieces. Using a potato peeler or sharp knife, make thin strips.

Place prepared rhubarb into the warm syrup. Use tongs, or your hands to toss the pieces in the syrup mixture to completely coat. Leave in the saucepan for 45 minutes.

Place a cookie rack over paper towel, parchment paper, or wax paper. Move the rhubarb to the cookie rack to drain off excess sugar water. Leave for 30 minutes, turning the rhubarb at the 15-minute mark.

Oven Method
Heat oven to 200 F (90 C). Place rhubarb on parchment paper lined cookie sheets. Spread out so pieces do not touch each other.
Bake for 2 to 4 hours. Starting at the 2-hour mark, check to determine leathery consistency (see Suggestions). Continue drying and checking until the desired consistency is met.
Turn off the oven. Leave rhubarb in the oven for at least one hour.

Dehydrator Method
Dehydrate for 4 to 6 hours at medium heat, or approximately 135 F (60 C).
Starting at the 4-hour mark, check to determine leathery consistency (see Suggestions). Continue drying and checking until the desired consistency is met.
Turn off the dehydrator. Leave rhubarb in the dehydrator for at least one hour.
For best results, follow manufacturer's instructions.

Suggestions

Leathery consistency is bendable and pliable, like fruit leather. It should not be brittle or stringy.

If the dehydrated pieces are too sticky to remove from the trays, place the trays in the freezer for at least 45 minutes. The rhubarb can then be removed from the trays using a spatula. Store in a sealed container in the freezer.

Storing in a sealable bag in the fridge may need additional moisture patted from the pieces with a paper towel.

Notes

Coconut Strawberry Popsicles

Ingredients

2 cups	Fresh Strawberries	500 mL
1 cup	Fresh Rhubarb	250 mL
1/4 cup	Pure Maple Syrup	60 mL
1 can	Full Fat Coconut Milk	400 mL
8 - 12	Popsicle Sticks	8 - 12

Directions

Cut rhubarb, strawberries into 1/4" (.635 cm) pieces. Place in a large saucepan and with maple syrup.

Bring to a boil over medium heat. Reduce heat to simmer until there are no chunks in the mixture. This takes about 15 minutes on the simmer setting. Help the process along by stirring every so often. Remove from heat and cool.

Fill popsicle molds 1/4 full with rhubarb mixture and freeze until it sets up. If it's not completely frozen solid, that's okay.

Add popsicle sticks. (See Suggestions)

Remove from freezer. Pour in a layer of coconut milk. Return to freezer until frozen.

Continue layering in this manner until the mold is filled. Add a popsicle stick. Return to freezer for 4 - 5 hours or until completely frozen.

Suggestions

If a commercial popsicle mold with sticks attached to the lid is **NOT** being used, add popsicle sticks before adding coconut milk.

For a smoother consistency, puree the rhubarb mixture after it has cooled.

After the first batch of rhubarb mixture and the layer of coconut milk has gone to the freezer, blend the remaining mixture with coconut milk to top off each popsicle mold. Freeze as directed.

Mix all of the rhubarb mixture and the coconut milk together. Fill each popsicle mold with the blended mixture. Freeze as directed.

Notes

Dip Sticks

Ingredients

1	Fresh Rhubarb	1
1/4 cup	Sugar	60 mL

Directions

Pull a stalk of rhubarb from the garden.

Remove the leaf.

Wash the stalk.

Cut the root end off of the stalks and trim a thin slice from the leaf end. This lets the rhubarb juice flow.

Dip either end of the stalk into the sugar and enjoy.

Suggestions

Too much fresh rhubarb might cause a tummy ache, especially for small children.

Cut the stalk into smaller pieces before handing them out with a bowl of sugar.

Notes

Gummy Treats

These Gummy Treats are more for adults, but, with a little change up, kids of every age will like them.

Ingredients

3/4 cup	Natural Fresh Fruit Juice	175 mL
3/4 cup	Rhubarb Stock	175 mL
4 tablespoons	Gelatin	60 mL
3 tablespoons	Honey	45 ml
1/4 teaspoon	Ginger	1 mL
1/2 teaspoon	Turmeric	2.5 mL

Directions

Mix the juice and rhubarb stock. Sprinkle gelatin over mixture (one tablespoon (15 mL) at a time. Whisk into juice until there are no lumps.

Heat the liquid over low heat until runny and gelatin has dissolved.

Remove from heat and stir in honey. Add ginger and turmeric, mixing until incorporated, and there are no lumps.

Pour into a 8" x 8" (20 x 20 cm) or 9" x 9" (22 x 22 cm) cake pan.

Refrigerate until liquid sets, at least 30 minutes.

Cut into 1" squares (2.54 cm), store in a sealed container in the fridge.

Enjoy whenever you like. Serve direct from the fridge or at room temperature.

Suggestions

Fresh squeezed juice of your choice, such as apple, cherry, lemon, orange, peach, or pomegranate.

Four lemons make approximately 3/4 of a cup (175 mL) of juice.

Five packages of Knox™ gelatin equals four tablespoons (60 mL).

Use fresh Turmeric if possible.

Use peeled and finely grated fresh ginger, if possible.

Natural fruit juice comes in whatever your tastebuds demand - cherry, orange, peach, apple, rhubarb.

Omit the ginger and turmeric to make a tasty treat for any age.

Notes

Leather

Ingredients

2 cups	Rhubarb	500 mL
1 tablespoon	Water	15 mL
1 tablespoon	Sweetener - If Needed	15 mL

Directions

In a blender or food processor, puree rhubarb. Add water, 1 - 2 tablespoons (15 - 30 mL) to start puree process, if needed.

Add sweetener of choice, if needed.

If the rhubarb puree is too runny, puree one apple, adding approximately 3/4 cup (175 mL) to the rhubarb.

Place solid dehydrator sheet on a dehydrator rack. Pour the puree onto the solid sheet. Spread evenly 1/4" (.635 cm) to 3/8" (.9525 cm).

Drying may take 8 - 12 hours. The result should feel leather-like with no sticky spots on either the top or the bottom

While leather is still warm, cut and roll, or cut into pieces.

To store, wrap cooled leather in plastic wrap and place in an airtight and moisture proof container.

Suggestions

For best results, follow your dehydrator instructions.

Notes

DESSERTS

Rhubarb Charlotte

A little bit of elegance for the end of a meal.

Ingredients

1 tablespoon	Gelatin	15 mL
1/4 cup	Cold Water	60 mL
3 cups	Fresh Rhubarb	750 mL
1/2 cup	Water	125 mL
1 cup	Sugar	250 mL
1/2 teaspoon	Vanilla	2.5 mL
1/4 teaspoon	Almond Extract	1 mL
2/3 cup	Whipping Cream	150 mL

Directions

Mix gelatin and 1/4 cup (60 mL) of water together until smooth. Set aside.

Cut rhubarb into 1/2" (1.27 cm) pieces and combine with 1/2 cup (125 mL) of water and sugar in a saucepan. Bring to a boil, stirring until sugar is dissolved. Cover and simmer 12-15 minutes until the rhubarb is tender. Remove from heat.

Add gelatin, stirring until dissolved. Add vanilla and almond extract. Stir until combined.

Chill mixture until partially set.

Whip the whipping cream until stiff. Fold into chilled mixture.

Serve as is in small dessert bowls.

For a fancier serving presentation, use a spring-form pan. Place parchment paper on the bottom of the pan and line the edge with lady fingers. Fill with mixture. Chill until ready to serve. Remove from pan. Leave parchment paper in place. Move to a plate and slice.

In a deep-dish pie plate press Crumble Topping (recipe found in the Extras section) on the bottom and up the sides. Fill with charlotte mixture. Chill until ready to serve.

Suggestions

Notes

Cheesecake

Ingredients

Sauce

2 1/2 cups	Rhubarb	625 mL
1/3 cup	Sugar	75 mL
2 tablespoons	Orange Juice	30 mL

Crust

2 cups	Graham Crackers Crumbs	500 mL
1/3 cup	Butter - Melted	75 mL

Filling

3 - 8 oz packages	Cream Cheese-Softened	3 - 250 g
1 - 16 oz	Sour Cream	500 g
1/2 cup	Sugar	125 mL
1 tablespoon	Cornstarch	15 mL
2 teaspoons	Vanilla	10 mL
1/2 teaspoon	Salt	2.5 mL
3	Eggs	3
8 - 1 oz	White Baking Chocolate Squares	250 g

Directions

Preheat oven to 350 F (175 C).

Sauce - Thinly slice rhubarb and combine with sugar and orange juice in a saucepan. Bring to a boil, reduce heat, and continue to cook uncovered until the rhubarb is tender - about 5 minutes. Stir occasionally or the mixture may stick to the bottom of the pan and burn. Remove from heat. Set aside to cool. Reserve 1/2 cup (125 mL) of sauce to use for garnish.

Crust - Mix graham crackers with the melted butter. Using a 10" (25 cm) springform pan, press the crumb mixture on the bottom and 1 1/2" (3.8 cm) up the sides. Wrap the outside of the springform pan with foil. Either a double layer or heavy-duty foil will work.

Filling - In a saucepan, melt chocolate over very low heat, stirring constantly to a smooth consistency. Set aside to cool. This step can be done prior to making the crust to ensure the chocolate is cooled before adding to the sour cream mixture.

Use an electric mixer to blend together cream cheese, sour cream, sugar, cornstarch, vanilla and salt. This mixture needs to be well blended and smooth. Add eggs, one at a time. Beat only until combined after each egg is added. Slowly add in melted chocolate until combined.

Pour half of the filling into the pan. Spread 1 cup (250 mL) of the sauce evenly over the filling. Add the remaining filling, again spreading evenly. Finish with the remaining sauce, then gently swirl the sauce into the filling.

Place the springform pan into a roasting pan with at least 1" (2.54 cm) between the pan edges; put into the pre-heated oven. Carefully pour boiling water into the roasting pan until it reaches half way up the springform pan. Check the water level every half hour. Replenish as needed to keep the water height at the half way point on the springform pan.

Bake for 1 1/2 to 2 hours, until the edge of the cheesecake is firm and the centre looks like it is almost set.

Remove the springform pan from the water-filled roaster in the oven. Leave to cool on a wire rack for 15 minutes.

Remove the foil. Use a knife to loosen the cheesecake from the sides of the springform pan. Cool for at least another 30 minutes. DO NOT try and remove the springform pan before cooling time is up.

Remove the springform sides and cool completely. Cover with plastic wrap and chill in the fridge for 4 hours or more before serving.

Serve with whipped cream and drizzle with sauce.

Suggestions

For best results, use chocolate squares with cocoa butter.

Frozen rhubarb can be used if it is completely thawed and drained.

Use regular cream cheese, not light.

Use regular sour cream, not light.

Make ahead and store in the fridge for up to two days.

Notes

Honey Snake Fence

Ingredients

Crust

1 cup + 2 tablespoons	Flour	280 mL
1/2 teaspoon	Sugar	2.5 mL
Pinch	Salt	Pinch
1/4 cup + 2 tablespoons	Butter	90 mL
3 - 4 tablespoons	Water	45 - 60 mL

Filling

Step One

2 - 4 Stalks	Rhubarb	2 - 4
1 tablespoon + 1 teaspoon	Sugar	20 mL
1 tablespoon	Flour	15 mL

Step Two

1/2 cup	Slivered Almonds	125 mL
3 tablespoons	Mascarpone Cheese	45 mL
2 tablespoons	Honey	30 mL
1/2 teaspoon	Vanilla	2.5 mL

Egg Wash

1	Egg Yolk	1
1 tablespoon	Milk	15 mL

Finish

1 1/2 teaspoons	Honey - Heated to Warm Not Bubbly Hot	7.5 mL

Directions

Preheat oven to 400 F (200 C).

Crust - Combine flour, sugar, and salt. Add butter. Use a pastry cutter or your hands to mix to a fine crumble stage. Add three tablespoons (45 mL) of water. Mix with a fork. If the mixture seems dry and crumbly, add more water, one teaspoon (5 mL) at a time. The dough needs to resemble a biscuit dough. Lightly knead until dough forms a ball.

Remove dough from bowl and flatten to resemble a 1" (2.54 cm) thick square. Wrap in plastic wrap and chill in the fridge for at least one hour.

Filling - Cut rhubarb into 3" (7.5 cm) lengths. Cut each of these lengths into several 1/4" (0.635 cm) strips. Place in a bowl and combine with sugar and flour. Set aside.

Toast almonds. Using a food processor, pulse almonds until finely ground. Do not over process or you will end up with almond butter.

Place almonds, mascarpone cheese, honey, and vanilla in a bowl. Mix together until well combined and smooth. Set aside.

Egg Wash - In a small bowl, mix together beaten egg yolk and milk to make an egg wash. Set aside. Whisk again before using.

Remove the dough from fridge. Let it sit at room temperature for 5 minutes. Lightly flour your work surface and roll dough out to a 14" square (35 cm). Move the dough to a parchment paper lined baking pan.

Leave a 2 1/2" (6.35 cm) border, spread the mascarpone mixture evenly over the dough.

Place rhubarb on top in a snake fence design. You may need to cut rhubarb down to size to fit the size of the pan and to make the pattern.

Fold the edges of the dough over the rhubarb. Pinch edges like you would for a pie crust. Brush crust with egg wash.

Bake for 40 - 45 minutes. The crust should be a golden brown. Remove from oven. Finish by brushing with warmed honey. Serve immediately plain or with whipped cream or ice cream.

Suggestions

The number of rhubarb stalks needed will be determined by the length and thickness of your stalks.

A snake fences look like a military chevron insignia, or zig-zag design.

Notes

Sweet Rolls

Quick, easy and oh so good.

Ingredients

1 - 8 tube	Crescent Rolls	1 - 8 tube
1/2 cup	Butter	125 mL

Filling

1 to 1 1/3 cups	Rhubarb	250 - 325 mL
1/2 cup	Sugar	125 mL
1/4 cup	Water	60 mL
1 teaspoon	Cornstarch	5 mL
1/2 teaspoon	Vanilla	2.5 mL

Glaze

1 tablespoon	Butter - Melted	15 mL
2/3 cup	Powdered Sugar	150 mL
1/2 teaspoon	Vanilla	2.5 mL
2 tablespoons	Heavy Cream	30 mL

Directions

Chop rhubarb into 1/4" (.635 cm) pieces.

Filling - In a nonstick skillet, combine 1/2 cup (125 mL) sugar with 1/4 cup (60 mL) water. Cook over medium heat until sugar dissolves. Add the rhubarb and simmer until very thick, about 10 minutes. Mash the rhubarb with a fork and scrape down the skillet sides. Fold in cornstarch and vanilla extract. Remove from heat and set aside to cool.

When ready to continue, preheat oven to 350 F (175 C).

On top of a piece of parchment paper, carefully unroll crescent rolls into a rectangle. Press together seams of all eight rolls to get a smooth surface. Spread a small amount of softened butter over the dough surface.

Spread out 1/2 cup (125 mL) of filling from in the middle of the dough. Make sure to leave 1 inch (2.54 cm) border on all sides.

Starting at the short end, tightly roll the dough back into a roll, pressing together seams as needed. Slice into eight rolls and place on a parchment lined baking sheet. Bake for about 10 minutes or until browned. Prepare glaze.

Glaze - In a small bowl, whisk butter, powdered sugar, vanilla extract, and heavy cream. Drizzle onto hot rolls.

Suggestions

Notes

Tapioca Pudding

Tapioca is one of my favourite desserts. Adding rhubarb takes it up another notch.

Ingredients

3 cups	Fresh Rhubarb	750 mL
2 cups	Water	500 mL
1/2 cup	Tapioca - Quick Cook	125 mL
2 pinches	Salt	2 pinches
2 teaspoons	Fresh Orange Zest	10 mL

Directions

Cut rhubarb into 1/4" to 1/2" (.635 cm to 1.27cm) pieces.

Place water in a saucepan. Bring to a boil. Add tapioca and salt. Continue cooking, and stirring, over low heat for about 5 minutes or until thickened.

Add rhubarb and continue cooking for about 10 minutes. Stir occasionally. Add sugar and orange zest, stir until sugar is dissolved.

Cool before serving with ice cream or whipped cream.

Suggestions

Replace fresh orange zest with one teaspoon (5 mL) dried.

Notes

Homestead Vegetables - Rhubarb

HOME PRESERVES

Hints for Canning and Preserving.

- The preference to use a hot water bath in making preserves is at the discretion of the maker. Processing time will be determined by altitude. Results may not be as expected. Not all preserves require additional processing.

- Quantity of rhubarb stalks needed will depend on how many jars you want to make and the length of the stalks.

- Use a clean knife to remove air bubbles. Slide the blade down the inside of the jar's edge and make a figure eight.

- Whenever possible, use fresh rhubarb, preferably harvested on the day it is to be used.

- Wipe rims of jars with a clean cloth, and seal with lids.

- Recipes that do not require processing the filled jars in a hot water bath or pressure cooker can be cooled on the counter until the popping sound indicates the jars are sealed.

- To freeze rhubarb for future use, remove the leaf, wash, and cut into the desired size. Spread out on a parchment paper lined cookie sheet. Freeze. Remove from cookie sheet. Measure 1-2 cup (250-500 mL) bag or container portions. Return to freezer.

- Dehydrate rhubarb by following the manufacturer's instructions for your dehydrating machine.

- The process of sealing jars with lids & rings is completed by tighten the rings with gentle twist using your fingers. This is called finger tightening. The rings should not be used to cinch down tight as this can damage the seal on the lid, and may cause the jar may not seal properly.

- Prepare jars and lids by sterilizing them with boiling water. Jars and lids should be hot to touch when being filled with preserves.

- Skimming removes froth from the top of the boiling jams and jellies. By adding butter to the boiling mixture, this reduces the amount of skimming required.

- Keep the skimmed-off mixture. It makes a tasty jam-like product.

Apple Rhubarb Jam

Ingredients

3 cups	Rhubarb	750 mL
3 cups	Apple	750 mL
2 cups	Sugar	500 mL
1/2 cups	Water	125 mL
1 tablespoon	Ground Cinnamon	15 mL
1/2 teaspoon	Ground Nutmeg	2.5 mL
1 - 2 oz pkg	Dry Pectin	57 g
1/2 teaspoon	Butter	2.5 mL
8 (+/-) 1/2 pint	Jars	8 (+/-) 125 mL

Directions

Prepare jars and lids.

Wash and dice rhubarb into into 1/4" (.635 cm) pieces.

Peel, core, and dice apples into into 1/4" (.635 cm) pieces.

In a large saucepan, combine rhubarb, apples, sugar, water, cinnamon, and nutmeg. On a medium-high heat, bring to boil, constantly stirring until sugar is dissolved. Reduce heat to medium and continue boiling. Stirring occasionally, approximately 20 minutes, or until rhubarb and apples have softened.

Stir in the pectin and boil for 5 minutes.

Remove from heat. Stir in butter. This will reduce the amount of skimming that may be needed.

Place jam in hot, sterilized jars, leaving 1/2" (1.27 cm) headroom.

Wipe rims of jars with a clean cloth, and seal with sterilized lids. Finger tighten the rings.

Process in a boiling water bath for 10 minutes.

Remove from bath and cool on the counter until the popping sound indicates the jars are sealed.

Suggestions

Quantity of rhubarb stalks needed will depend on how many jars you want to make and the length of the stalks.

For added flavour, use fresh grated nutmeg.

Once rhubarb and apples have softened, use a potato masher to reduce the size of pieces.

Notes

Onion Rhubarb Relish

Ingredients

5 cups	Rhubarb	1.25 L
5 cups	Onion	1.25 L
2 1/2 cups	Apple Cider Vinegar	625 mL
6 cups	Brown Sugar - Packed	1.5 L
1 tablespoon	Salt	15 mL
1 teaspoon	Ground Pepper	5 mL
1 teaspoon	Ground Cinnamon	5 mL
1 teaspoon	Ground Cloves	5 mL
5 - 7 (+/-) 1/2 pint	Jars	5 - 7 (+/-) 125 mL

Directions

Prepare jars and lids.

Wash and cut up rhubarb into 1/2" (1.27 cm) pieces, and chop onions into 1/4" (.635 cm) pieces.

Place rhubarb, onions, and vinegar in a large saucepan. Bring to a boil over medium heat. Cook uncovered for about 20 minutes. The onions should be tender. Stir often to help break down the mixture.

Add brown sugar, salt, pepper, cinnamon, and cloves. Continue to cook until thick, about 30 - 45 minutes. Stir often.

Remove from heat. Place mixture in hot, sterilized jars to 1/2" (1.27 cm) from the top.

Use a clean knife to remove air bubbles. Slide the blade down the inside of the jar's edge and make a figure eight.

Wipe rims of jars with a clean cloth, and seal with sterilized lids. Finger tighten the rings.

Let cool on the counter until the popping sound indicates the jars are sealed.

Suggestions

Quantity of rhubarb stalks needed will depend on how many jars you want to make and the length of the stalks.

Notes

Pickling Rhubarb

Ingredients

2 - 3 Stalks	Fresh Rhubarb	2 - 3 Stalks
1 1/2 cups	Water	375 mL
3/4 cup	Apple Cider Vinegar	175 mL
1 tablespoon	Sugar	15 mL
1 tablespoon	Salt	15 mL
2 - 3 one pint	Jars	2 -3 250 mL

Directions

Prepare jars and lids.

Wash and cut rhubarb to fit into jars. Cut into 1/2" (1.27 cm) pieces, or leave in lengths the size of the jars. Either way, leave 1" (2.54 cm) of headroom when filling jars.

Place water, vinegar, sugar, and salt in a saucepan. Bring to a boil and continue cooking until sugar and salt have dissolved.

While vinegar mixture is cooking, pack rhubarb pieces into hot jars.

Pour vinegar mixture over rhubarb, leaving 1/2" (1.27 cm) headroom to the top of the jar.

Wipe rims of jars with a clean cloth, and seal with sterilized lids. Finger tighten the rings.

Cool on the counter until the popping sound indicates the jars are sealed.

Store in a cool location for 4 - 6 weeks before using.

Suggestions

For smaller portions, substitute with four half pint jars (125 mL).

Quantity of rhubarb stalks needed will depend on how many jars you want to make and the length of the stalks.

For best results, use firm rhubarb stalks.

Harvest and use the rhubarb on the same day pickles are to be made.

Notes

Rhubarb Jelly

Ingredients

1 3/4 cups	Rhubarb Stock	425 mL
3 1/2 cups	Sugar	875 mL
1 pouch	Liquid Pectin	85 mL
1/2 teaspoon	Butter	2.5 mL
3 (+/-) 1/2 pint	Jars	3 (+/-) 125 mL

Directions

Prepare jars and lids.

Combine rhubarb stock and sugar in a large saucepan. Mix well. Cook over high heat until mixture comes to a boil. Stir continually.

Add pectin and bring to a full rolling boil. Boil hard for one minute, stirring constantly.

Remove from heat. Stir in butter. This will reduce the amount of skimming needed.

Pour jelly into hot, prepared jars to about 1/2" (1.27 cm) from the rim.

Use a clean knife to remove air bubbles. Slide the blade down the inside of the jar's edge and make a figure eight.

Wipe rims of jars with a clean cloth, and seal with sterilized lids. Finger tighten the rings.

Cool on the counter until the popping sound indicates the jars are sealed.

Suggestions

Rhubarb Stock recipe can be found in the Beverage section.

Notes

Rhubarb Marmalade

Ingredients

4 1/2 cups	Fresh Rhubarb	1 L
4 1/2 cups	Sugar	1L
1 1/2	Oranges	1 1/2
5 (+/-) 1/2 pint	Jars	5 (+/-) 125 mL

Directions

Place a saucer in the freezer.

Prepare jars and lids.

Wash and cut rhubarb into 1/2" (1.27 cm) pieces

Remove the peel from the oranges and remove the pith from the peel. Slice peel into thin strips—toothpick width.

Remove any additional pith left on the peeled oranges. Slice oranges into 1/4" (.635 cm) pieces. Dice into smaller pieces.

In a large saucepan, combine rhubarb, sugar, oranges, and orange peel. Mix well.

Bring to a boil over medium-high heat. Continue to boil, uncovered for at least 30 minutes, stirring occasionally.

Remove saucer from freezer and place a small spoonful of marmalade mixture on it. If it jells, the marmalade is ready to put into jars. If it doesn't jell, put the saucer back in the freezer and continue cooking for 2 minutes before you test again. Keep testing at 2-minute intervals until the jell consistency is reached.

Fill hot, sterilized jars to within 1/4" (.635 cm) from the top. Cover with sterilized lids. Finger tighten the rings. Leave on the counter to cool. When you hear the sound of the pop of the lids the jars have sealed. Store in a cool location until you are ready to use.

Suggestions

Notes

Salsa - Rhubarb Style

Ingredients

2 cups	Fresh Rhubarb	500 mL
1/2 cup	Red Sweet Pepper	125 mL
1/2 cup	Yellow Sweet Pepper	125 mL
1/2 cup	Fresh Cilantro	125 mL
3	Green Onions	3
1	Hot Pepper of Choice	1
2 tablespoons	Fresh Lime Juice	30 mL

Brown Sugar, Salt, Fresh Ground Pepper

Directions

Finely chop rhubarb. Set aside.

Finely chop cilantro. Set aside.

Finely chop green onions. Set aside.

Finely chop red and yellow pepper. Set aside.

Remove seeds from hot pepper and finely chop. Set aside.

Blanch rhubarb in boiling water for 10 seconds. Remove from heat, strain. Plunge rhubarb into cold water for 15 seconds. Drain well.

Place all chopped vegetables in a glass bowl. Sprinkle with lime juice and toss.

Add brown sugar, salt, and fresh ground pepper to taste.

Cover and place fridge for 1 hour before serving. Makes about 2 cups (500 mL).

Suggestions

Hot peppers come in many heat levels. It's your choice as to which one you will incorporate into this recipe. Use latex or rubber gloves when handling hot peppers.

Do not use a plastic bowl to mix the ingredients or a plastic container in which to store leftovers. The hot pepper flavour will permeate into the containers and may not be removable when cleaned.

Notes

Saskatoon Rhubarb Jam

Ingredients

1 large	Orange	1 large
1 large	Lemon	1 large
12 cups	Rhubarb	3 L
7 1/2 cups	Saskatoons	1.875 L
6 cup	Sugar	1.42 L
1/2 teaspoon	Butter	2.5 mL
8 (+/-) 1/2 pint	Jars	8 (+/-) 125 mL

Directions

Prepare jars and lids.

Wash and dice rhubarb into 1/4" (.635 cm) pieces.

Peel orange, remove all pith, and dice.

Squeeze juice from lemon. Set aside.

In a large saucepan, combine orange, sugar, and rhubarb. On medium-high heat, bring to a boil, constantly stirring until sugar is dissolved. Reduce heat to medium and continue boiling, occasionally stirring, until mixture thickens.

Add saskatoons and lemon juice. Bring mixture back to a rolling boil. Continue boiling, frequently stirring, until mixture has reduced and is thick, about 15 -20 minutes. Remove from heat. Stir in butter. This will reduce the amount of skimming that may be needed.

Place jam in hot, sterilized jars, leaving 1/4" (.635 cm) headroom.

Wipe rims of jars with a clean cloth, and seal with sterilized lids. Finger tighten the rings.

Process in a boiling water bath for 10 minutes. Remove from bath and cool on the counter until the popping sound indicates the jars are sealed.

Suggestions

Quantity of rhubarb stalks needed will depend on how many jars you want to make and the length of the stalks.

Notes

Strawberry Rhubarb Compote

Ingredients

6 cups	Strawberries	1.5 L
1	Orange	1
2 cups	Rhubarb	500 mL
1 cup	Raisins	250 mL
1/4 cup	Lemon Juice	60 mL
1 cup	Pecans (Optional)	250 mL
8 (+/-) 1/2 pint	Jars	8 (+/-) 125 mL

Sugar is needed for this recipe. The amount is based on the number of cups (mL) the rhubarb mixture makes.

Directions

Prepare jars and lids.

Wash, hull and cut strawberries into quarters.

Scrub orange. Do not peel. Chop finely by hand, or use a food processor.

Wash and dice rhubarb into into 1/4" (.635 cm) pieces.

Coarsely chop the pecans.

Mix strawberries, orange, rhubarb, raisins, and lemon juice together in a bowl.

Move the mixture to a large saucepan by the cup full. **Record the number of cups of mixture measured**. This will determine the amount of sugar needed.

Measure out 3/4 cup (175 mL) of sugar for each cup of mixture. Set sugar aside.

Place rhubarb mixture over medium-high heat. Gradually add sugar. To prevent scorching continue to stir until mixture boils.

Boil uncovered for 30 - 45 minutes until mixture reaches gel stage.

If including nuts, add them now, and boil for one more minute.

Remove from heat. Place mixture in hot, sterilized jars, leaving 1/2" (1.27cm) headroom.

Use a clean knife to remove air bubbles. Slide the blade down the inside of the jar's edge and make a figure eight.

Wipe rims of jars with a clean cloth, and seal with sterilized lids. Finger tighten the rings.

Let cool on the counter until the popping sound indicates the jars are sealed.

Suggestions

Quantity of rhubarb stalks needed will depend on how many jars you want to make and the length of the stalks.

Read helpful hints regarding processing preserves.

Replace strawberries with pears or plums or a mixture of both.

Replace raisins for craisins or a mixture of both.

Notes

Strawberry Rhubarb Jam

Ingredients

2 cups	Strawberries	500 mL
2 cups	Rhubarb - Diced	500 mL
5 1/2 cups	Sugar	1.3 L
1/4 cup	Lemon Juice	60 mL
1 pouch	Liquid Pectin	85 mL
1/2 teaspoon	Butter	2.5 mL
4 - 6 (+/-) 1/2 pint	Jars	4 - 6 (+/-) 125 mL

Directions

Prepare jars and lids.

Wash, hull, and mash strawberries. There should be no large chunks.

Wash and dice rhubarb into 1/4" (.635 cm) pieces.

In a large saucepan, mix together strawberries and rhubarb, add lemon juice and pectin. Mix well. Cook over medium heat until mixture starts to boil and make its own juice.

Add sugar, 1 cup (250 mL) at a time. Stir each addition until sugar is dissolved.

Let mixture return to a rolling boil. Boil hard for one minute, stir constantly.

Remove from heat. Stir in butter. This will reduce the amount of skimming needed.

Place jam in hot, sterilized jars.

Wipe rims of jars with a clean cloth, and seal with sterilized lids. Finger tighten the rings.

Cool on the counter until the popping sound indicates the jars are sealed.

Suggestions

Quantity of rhubarb stalks needed will depend on how many jars you want to make and the length of the stalks.

Notes

Homestead Vegetables - Rhubarb

PIE

Dandelion Rhubarb Pie

Who would have thought the invasive, yellow flowers dotting the landscape in spring and summer would be an ideal addition to a pie!

Ingredients

1	9" (22 cm) Single Pie Crust - Unbaked	1
1	Crumble Topping Recipe	
3 cups	Fresh Rhubarb	750 mL
1/2 cup	Dandelion Flowers	125 mL
2	Eggs	2
1 1/2 cups	Sugar	625 mL
1 1/2 teaspoons	Vanilla	7.5 mL
3 tablespoons	Flour	45 mL
1	Crumble Topping Recipe	1

Directions

Preheat Oven to 400 F (200 C).

Make Crumble Topping - recipe found in Extras section.

Cut rhubarb into 1/2" (1.27 cm) pieces.

Harvest dandelions. DO NOT use flowers that have been sprayed with any kind of pesticides. Wash flowers to remove any bugs and dirt. Remove green base and stem from flowers - these will give a bitter taste if left on. Break flowers apart and fluff to measure 1/2 cup (125 mL). Mix with rhubarb.

In a bowl, beat eggs, add vanilla, sugar, and flour. Pour over rhubarb mixture and stir until well coated. Place mixture into the pie crust and sprinkle with Crumble Topping.

Bake for 10 minutes at 400 F (200 C). Reduce heat to 350 F (175 C) and continue baking for 35 - 40 minutes or until crust is golden brown and rhubarb is soft. Allow pie to cool for 10 minutes before cutting.

Suggestions

Notes

Custard Rhubarb Pie

An oldie but a goodie.

Ingredients

1	9" (22 cm) Double Pie Crust - Unbaked	1
3 cups	Rhubarb	750 mL
1 cup	Sugar	250 mL
2 tablespoons	Flour	30 mL
1/2 cup	Light Cream	125 mL
2	Eggs	2
1/4 teaspoon	Salt	1 mL
1 teaspoon	Vanilla	5 mL

Directions

Preheat oven to 450 F (230 C).

Cut rhubarb into 1/2" (1.27 cm) pieces.

Mix the rhubarb with 1/2 cup (125 mL) of sugar and the flour. Place in an unbaked pie crust.

Mix together 2 eggs, 1/2 cup (125 mL) of sugar, salt, cream, and vanilla. Pour over rhubarb.

Cover with top crust, seal and trim edges with a sharp knife. Make two 1" (2.54 cm) slashes on the top of the crust to allow the seam to escape while cooking.

Bake 15 minutes at 450 F (230 C). Reduce to 350 F (175C). Continue baking for another 30 minutes.

Suggestions

Notes

Humble Rhubarb Pie

Humble Pie made with rhubarb is a bit of an oddity as most recipes that go by this name have fillings made from animal parts. Rhubarb's humble beginnings fits this recipe.

Ingredients

1	9" (22 cm) Single Pie Crust - Unbaked	1
2 1/2 cups	Fresh Rhubarb	625 mL
2 cups	Water	500 mL
2	Eggs	2
1 cup	Evaporated Milk	250 mL
1/4 cup	Sugar	60 mL
1 1/2 teaspoons	Vanilla	7.5 mL
2 tablespoons	Flour	30 mL
1/2 teaspoon	Nutmeg	2.5 mL
2 tablespoons	Butter - Melted and Cooled	30 mL

Directions

Preheat oven to 350 F (175 C).

Dice rhubarb into into 1/4" (.635 cm) pieces.

Filling - Bring rhubarb and water to a boil in a medium saucepan. Reduce heat and simmer for 3 minutes. Remove from heat and let stand for 2 minutes. Strain through a jelly bag or cheesecloth. Reserve juice. Spread rhubarb pulp evenly into pie crust.

Topping - In a bowl, mix eggs, milk, sugar, and vanilla. Sprinkle flour and nutmeg over the egg mixture and blend in. Add melted butter, beating until all ingredients are blended and smooth. Slowly pour mixture over rhubarb.

Cover pie with foil and bake for 25 minutes. Remove foil and continue baking for another 15 to 20 minutes or until centre is almost set. Remove from oven and let stand for 20 to 30 minutes before cutting.

Suggestions

For added flavour, use freshly grated nutmeg.
Notes

Old Fashioned Rhubarb Pie

Ingredients

Pie

1	9" (22 cm) Double Pie Crust - Unbaked	1
4 cups	Rhubarb	1 L
1 1/4 - 1 3/4 cups	Sugar	310 - 425 mL
1/3 cup	Flour	75 mL
1 pinch	Salt	1 pinch
1 tablespoon	Butter	15 mL

Milk and sugar for glazing.

Directions

Preheat oven to 400 F (200 C).

Cut rhubarb into 1/4" to 1/2" (.635 to 1.27 cm) pieces.

In a bowl, mix flour, salt, and sugar together.

Place half of the rhubarb into the pie shell. Sprinkle with half of the flour mixture. Add the rest of the rhubarb followed by the rest of the flour mixture. Dot with butter. Cover with top crust. Seal and trim edges. With a sharp knife make a two 1" (2.53 cm) slashes on the top crust to allow steam to escape while cooking. Brush the top with milk. Add a dusting of sugar.

Place on a baking sheet and bake for 40 to 50 minutes until the pastry is nicely browned.

Remove from oven and allow pie to sit for 20 minutes before cutting.

Serve with ice cream.

Suggestions

The amount of sugar used will depend on how sweet or tart the rhubarb is AND how sweet you want the result to be.

Notes

Rhubarb Meringue Pie

This is a nice alternative for dessert.

Ingredients

Pie

1	9" (22 cm) Single Pie Crust - Unbaked	1
1 1/3 cups	Fresh Rhubarb	325 mL
3	Eggs	3
3/4 cup	Sugar	175 mL
1/8 teaspoon	Salt	.5 ml
1/2 teaspoon	Vanilla	2.5 mL
1 2/3 cups	Evaporated Milk	400 mL

Meringue

2	Egg Whites	2
1/8 teaspoon	Salt	.5 ml
1/4 cup	Sugar	60 mL

Directions

Preheat oven to 425 F (220 C).

Cut rhubarb into 1/4" to 1/2" (.635 to 1.27 cm) pieces.

Separate two eggs. Set whites aside. In a separate bowl, add yolks to the third egg and beat together. Add sugar, salt, vanilla, evaporated milk, and rhubarb. Pour into unbaked pie shell and bake at 425 F (220 C) for 20 minutes. Reduce oven heat to 350 F (175 C). Bake until custard is set, approximately 20 minutes more.

While pie is baking, prepare the meringue by beating the two egg whites with salt until foamy. Continue to beat, adding sugar a little at a time until stiff peaks form.

Remove the pie from the oven. Reduce heat to 325 F (165 C). Spread meringue over the hot pie, taking it to the edge of the pastry. This will seal it and prevent the meringue from shrinking as it bakes.

Return to the oven until the meringue is brown.

Remove the pie from the oven and cool before serving.

Suggestions

Hot pie filling helps to cook the meringue from underneath and prevents weeping. For best results, make the meringue as close to the time it is needed as possible.

Notes

Sour Cream Rhubarb Pie

Ingredients

Filling

1	9" (22 cm) Single Pie Crust - Unbaked	1
4 cups	Rhubarb	1 L
1	Egg	1
1 1/2 cups	Sugar	375 mL
1 cup	Sour Cream	250 mL
1/3 cup	Flour	75 mL

Topping

1/2 cup	Flour	125 mL
1/2 cup	Brown Sugar - Packed	125 mL
1/4 cup	Butter - Melted	60 mL

Directions

Preheat oven to 450 F (230 C).

Cut rhubarb into 1/4" (.635 cm) pieces.

Topping - In a small bowl mix the flour and brown sugar. Add the melted butter evenly over flour mixture. Use a fork or your hands to mix until a crumbly mixture forms. Set aside.

Place the rhubarb evenly in the bottom of the uncooked pie shell.

Filling - In a bowl, blend the egg, sugar, and sour cream until smooth. Slowly add the flour to the sour cream mixture. Stir after each addition of flour until blended and smooth. Pour over the rhubarb.

Evenly sprinkle the topping mixture over the sour cream and rhubarb filling.

Bake at 450 F (230 C) for 15 minutes. Reduce heat to 350 F (175 C) and continue to bake for approximately 40 minutes. The topping should be nicely browned and the edges of the pie will be puffed up. It is okay for the centre to be jiggly, but only a little.

Cool completely before serving.

Suggestions

Use a deep-dish pie shell, homemade or commercial.

Wrap edges of pie crust with foil when you reduce the heat. This will alleviate overcooking.

Check on the topping every so often. If it looks like it has browned enough, cover the pie with loosely fitting foil.

Notes

Strawberry Rhubarb Pie

Ingredients

Pie

1	9" (22 cm) Double Pie Crust - Unbaked	1
2 1/2 cups	Rhubarb	625 mL
2 1/2 cups	Strawberries	625 mL
1 cup	Sugar	250 mL
1/3 cup	Flour	75 mL
2 tablespoons	Butter	30 mL
1 teaspoon	Lemon Zest	5 mL

Glaze

1	Egg Yolk - Beaten	1
1 teaspoon	Water	5 ml

Directions

Preheat oven to 450 F (230 C).

Cut rhubarb into 1/4" to 1/2" (.635 to 1.27 cm) pieces. Hull and slice strawberries into 1/4" (.635 cm) pieces.

Mix flour, lemon zest, and sugar together.

Mix strawberries and rhubarb together. Add flour mixture. Toss to coat.

Place rhubarb mixture into the pie shell. Dot with butter. Cover with top crust. Seal and trim edges. With a sharp knife make a two 1" (2.54 cm) slashes on the top crust to allow steam to escape while cooking.

Glaze - 1 beaten egg yolk combined with 1 teaspoon (5 mL) water. Brush pie with glaze.

Place on a baking sheet. Bake for 15 minutes at 450 F (230 C). Reduce heat to 350 F (175 C). Bake for 30 minutes until the pastry is nicely browned. Remove from the oven and allow the pie to cool before cutting.

Suggestions

Notes

Homestead Vegetables - Rhubarb

Hints

Measurement Conversions

Recipes

Gardening

Hints for the Kitchen

- The recipes in this book have been baked and tested at 3600 feet (1098m) above sea level. Be sure to adjust your baking time to your location.

- The recipes in this book use all-purpose flour unless otherwise noted.

- The recipes in the book use butter unless otherwise noted.

- Make sure all ingredients are at room temperature. Butter should be soft. Eggs can be placed in warm water (not boiling) for 10 minutes to bring them to room temperature.

- Leavening agents (baking soda and baking powder) should be replaced yearly. To test their freshness, drop one teaspoon (5 mL) of baking powder into ½ cup (125 mL) hot water, or 1 teaspoon (5 mL) of baking soda into ¼ cup (60 mL) vinegar. If they don't bubble, your product is stale and needs to be replaced.

- Chilling cookie dough (an hour in the fridge, or 20 minutes in the freezer) will give cookies more rise and body.

- To keep cookies soft, store them in an airtight container.

- Make cookies as close to the same size as possible – this ensures they will all be done baking at the same time.

- Fresh ingredients make a difference! Ground spices lose their potency and flavour over time. If you can't remember the last time you bought cinnamon or cloves, it may be time to purchase a fresh container.

- Gently spoon flour into the measuring cup to avoid compacting. Level it off with the straight edge of a butter knife.

- To soften butter, leave it on the counter for a few hours before starting. If you are short on time, frozen butter can be grated into a bowl – it will soften in 10-15 minutes.

- Melon ballers or small ice cream scoops make forming drop cookies quick and easy.

- Baking sheets should be cool when placing dough on them. To cool a cookie sheet that was already in the oven, run it under cool water for 15-20 seconds. Dry before using again.

- To make soft cookies, remove them from the oven a minute or two early. Let them rest on the baking sheet for a few minutes, though. They will still look unbaked in the centre, (this is the secret) but will set up as they cool.

- When melting chocolate, it is recommended to use a double boiler instead of a microwave or stovetop. If the chocolate gets too hot while melting it will turn white or have white streaks in it once it cools.

- To keep cookies from falling apart when you move them from the baking sheet to a cooling rack, let them sit on the cookie sheet for 1 minute.

Our family and its history are an important part of our day to day way of life. Using recipes from several different eras has required us to know the terminology of the time.

CONVERSION CHARTS

Rhubarb

How do you tell the equivalent measure of one rhubarb stalk?
The information is calculated after the leaves have been trimmed.

4 large or 8 small stalks
= approximately 1 pound (500 g)
= approximately 4 cups (1 L) of 1" (1.27cm) pieces.
= approximately 2 cups (500 mL) cooked

1 small to medium stalk
= approximately 1/2 cup (125 mL) of 1" (1.27 cm) pieces
= approximately 2 tablespoons (30 mL) cooked puree - no sugar or liquid added

Oven Temperatures

Warm Oven	300 - 325 F	150 - 160 C
Moderate Oven	350 - 375 F	175 - 190 C
Hot Oven	400 - 425 F	205 - 220 C

Spoons

Conventional	Metric
1/4 teaspoon	1 mL
1/2 teaspoon	2.5 mL
1 teaspoon	5 mL
2 teaspoons	10 mL
1 tablespoon	15 mL

Cups

Conventional	Metric
1/4 cup	60 mL
1/3 cup	75 mL
1/2 cup	125 mL
2/3 cup	150 mL
3/4 cup	175 mL
1 cup	250 mL
4 1/2 cups	1 L

Buttery Liqueur Sauce

Ingredients

1/2 cup	Brown Sugar - Packed	125 mL
1/2 cup	Butter	125 mL
1/2 cup	Whipping Cream	125 mL
2 tablespoons	Liqueur or Brandy	30 mL

Directions

Combine brown sugar, butter, and whipping cream in a saucepan. Stir over medium heat until the sugar is dissolved and the butter is completely melted.

Reduce heat. Boil gently without stirring for about 5 minutes. You should notice that the mixture thickens.

Remove from heat, stir in liqueur or brandy and let stand for 10 minutes. It will continue to thicken as it cools.

Serve warm over your favourite cake.

Suggestions

For best results, use heavy whipping cream.

We like to use Kahlua™ in our sauce.

This recipe makes approximately 1 cup (250 mL) and can be easily doubled (recommended).

It is very rich, but oh so worth it! Any leftover sauce can be stored in the fridge for about three weeks. Warm over low heat before using.

Notes

Crumble Topping

Crumble Topping is the perfect keep-on-hand, dessert starter for the unexpected times when company stops by, or you feel like having something sweet.

Ingredients

1/2 cup	Butter - Chilled	125 mL
1/2 cup	Brown Sugar - Packed	125 mL
3/4 cup	Flour	175 mL
1/4 teaspoon	Ground Cinnamon	1 mL
1/4 teaspoon	Ground Cloves	1 mL

Directions

In a large bowl, mix the flour, cinnamon, cloves, and sugar. Add the cubed butter and blend the mixture until it has a crumbly consistency.

Suggestions

Spread 3 to 4 cups (750 mL to 1 L) of Crumble Topping over any kind of fruit. Bake at 350 F (175 C) for 30 - 40 minutes. Serve with ice cream or whipped cream. Makes 6 to 8 servings.

Spread 1/2 cup (125 mL) over any kind of fruit to make an individual serving. Bake at 350 F (175 C) for 15 - 20 minutes. Serve with ice cream or whipped cream.

The recipe can be doubled, or more, and kept in a sealed container in the fridge for use at any time.

Notes

Homestyle Vanilla

Ingredients

1 cup	Vodka	250 mL
6	Vanilla Beans	6

Directions

Cut vanilla beans into quarters. Do not scrape the beans, leave as is. Place in a clean glass jar with a tight-fitting lid.

Pour vodka over beans and seal.

Place out of direct sunlight and leave for a minimum of 4 - 6 weeks. Once a week, give it a shake.

Suggestions

Six vanilla beans will make the result quite strong. Reduce the number of beans to lower the strength to your taste.

Remove the beans or leave them in the vodka after the 6-week term to continue infusing the flavour.

Use whatever vodka you prefer. It does not have to be high end.

Notes

Old Fashioned Matrimonial Bars

These old favourites always showed up at teas and wedding showers.

Ingredients

Filling

1/2 pound block	Dates	.23 kg
1/2 cup	Water	125 mL
2 tablespoons	Brown Sugar	30 mL
1 teaspoon	Orange Zest	5 mL
1 teaspoon	Lemon Zest	5 mL
2 tablespoons	Orange Juice	30 mL

Crust

1 1/2 cups	Oats - Quick Cook	625 mL
1 1/2 cups	Flour	625 mL
1/2 teaspoon	Baking Soda	2.5 mL
1 teaspoon	Baking Powder	5 mL
1 pinch	Salt	1 pinch
1 cup	Brown Sugar	250 mL
1 cup	Butter	250 mL

Directions

Preheat over to 350 F (175 C).

Chop dates into 1/4" (.635 cm) pieces.

Filling - Combine dates, water, brown sugar, orange, and lemon zest, and orange juice in saucepan. Cook slowly over a medium heat until thick. Cool completely.

Crust - In a large bowl, blend oats, flour, baking soda, baking powder, salt, and brown sugar. Cube butter and add to oat mixture. Blend by hand or with a pastry cutter until crumbly.
Press 2/3 of the mixture into a greased 9" x 9" (22 x 22 cm) baking pan. Add filling, sprinkle with remaining oat mixture, and bake for 30 to 35 minutes. Cool completely before cutting.
Freezes well.

Suggestions

Double the crust part of the recipe and make a batch of rhubarb filled bars. See Matrimonial Bars recipe in the Cakes, Cookies, Muffins & Squares section.

Notes

Pie Pastry

This is our all-time favourite pie crust.

Ingredients

5 1/2 cups	All-Purpose Flour	1.25 L
2 teaspoons	Salt	10 mL
1 pound	Lard	.454 kg
1 tablespoon	Vinegar	15 mL
1	Egg - Lightly Beaten	1
	Water	

Directions

In a large bowl, mix flour and salt. Cut in lard and blend by hand to resemble course oatmeal.

In a measuring cup, lightly beat egg and add vinegar. Add enough water to equal one cup of liquid. Pour into the flour mixture and blend with a fork. Divide into four equal parts for easier handling.

Roll out on a lightly floured surface to the desired pie size needed.

Makes three 9-inch (22 cm) double pie crusts.

Suggestions

Wrap unused dough in plastic wrap and then place in sealable bags. It will keep in the fridge for a few weeks if not needed right away.

For best results, we use Tenderflake™ lard.

Notes

Vinaigrette

A little bit of savoury sweetness for your salad.

Ingredients

1 - 16" piece	Rhubarb	1 - 42 cm
1/2 cup	Water	125 mL
2 tablespoons	Honey	30 mL
2 tablespoons	Red Wine	30 mL
2 teaspoons	Grainy Dijon Mustard	10 mL
1/4 cup	Extra Virgin Olive Oil	60 mL

Directions

Cut rhubarb into 1/2" (125 mL) pieces. Place in a medium saucepan and add a 1/2 cup (125mL) of water. Simmer for about 5 minutes or until very soft. Remove from heat. Cool.

Place rhubarb into a blender. Add honey, wine, and mustard. Pulse until smooth.

With blender set to a low a low blend setting, slowly add oil.

Suggestions

Serve at room temperature.

Store in fridge.

Notes

Sour Milk

Ingredients

1 cup	Milk	250 mL
1 tablespoon	Lemon Juice OR Vinegar OR Rhubarb Stock	15 mL

Directions

Pour the milk into a glass jar or measuring cup.

Add the lemon juice OR vinegar OR Rhubarb Stock. Stir.

Let the mixture sit at room temperature for 1 hour.

Stir, and it is ready to use.

Suggestions

Rule of thumb for storage, the fresher the milk used to make the sour milk, the longer any leftovers can be kept. The expiration date on the milk carton is a good indicator.

Stored sour milk needs to be stirred before using. Keep in a tightly sealed glass jar for no longer than a week.

Whole milk results in thicker sour milk.

Reduced fat milk is good to use for 'light' recipes.

Notes

Homestead Vegetables - Rhubarb

Hints for the Garden.

Harvest rhubarb by pulling the stalks. Cutting stalks will encourage pests on the open wound left behind. The plant will continue to try and feed the cut stalk, removing the needed nutrients for new growth. Pulling stalks cleans out the undergrowth, leaving room for and encouraging the new stalks to emerge.

Bug Spray

Use the rhubarb leaves cut from the stalks. Rinse leaves to remove any dirt or bugs.

Place leaves into a large stockpot. Cover with water and bring to a boil. Keep the water at a slow rolling boil for about 30 minutes.

Remove the leaves. Strain the liquid through cheesecloth or a jelly bag. This removes any leftover leaf pieces and sediment.

To use, dilute with water, or use full strength. The ratio for diluting is one part liquid with two parts water. Spray leaves of bug-infested plants. Remember to spray the underside as well.

Depending on the strength of the bug spray used, there may be some browning on some plant leaves, especially house plants. Test spray on plant to check if strength of spray needs to be adjusted.

We recommend wearing gloves while handling or using this spray. Washing your hands with soap and warm water after each handling.

ComfyCountryCreations.com

FORCING RHUBARB

For those who love to eat fresh rhubarb and are disappointed when the last stalks are harvested, pine no more for this spring and summer treat during the winter months. Rhubarb, like daffodils and hyacinth, can be forced to grow indoors during its off-season; it does need a minimal cool period.

Before the ground freezes, but after all the tops die back, dig up one or more plants. Choose plants that are about three years old; they seem to work well with this technique.

Place the rhubarb in tubs with soil around the roots. Cover with straw to prevent them from drying out. You want them to be able to freeze, so don't put a thick blanket of straw over them. Leave them outside for a couple of weeks in temperatures below 32 F (0 C).

After two weeks of wintery weather, bring them inside to a basement, greenhouse or heated garage where the ideal temperature is between 50 to 60 F (10 to 15 C).

There are three important factors that need to be followed for successful forcing of rhubarb:

1. Good ventilation is required to prevent mould.
2. Keep the soil moist, but not soggy.
3. Keep out light. Omitting light will ensure leaf growth is minimal and chlorophyll will fail to develop in the stalks, making them tender and juicy.

The first stalks should be ready for harvest in about four weeks and should continue to produce for three or four more weeks.

Once the harvest is complete, weather permitting, transplant the rhubarb back into the outdoor garden. These plants may not produce again for a few years. Don't get discouraged; they are just rejuvenating and will be back again to fill you with their pleasures.

NOTE:
For a continuous harvest, start additional plants at two or three-week intervals.

ComfyCountryCreations.com

RHUBARB

(Rheum rhabarbarum)

Rhubarb as we know it has relatives - R.palmatum and R.officinale. Both of the relatives were highly sought after and valued by ancient customs, as a laxative. Their recorded use shows up around 2700 BC in China. It is thought that roots were probably brought to Europe via the Silk Route and by the end of the 13th century, Marco Polo reported it growing in China.

Can you imagine anyone claiming rhubarb mania?

Historians claim that Europe fit that description by the 18th century. Inside the borders of Russia, there was a trade monopoly happening and not to be outdone, the British East India Company bought roots in China. Up to this point, the plants had been used as an herb. It would appear that our rheum rhabarbarum became popular as a food by 1830; stalks were forced to be available year-round in the farmer's markets of the time.

As many would believe, rhubarb is not a fruit, but a vegetable. Depending on the variety, the stalks can vary in color from green to deep red. It contains a good source of potassium calcium and moderate amounts of vitamins A, and C. As well, it is low in calories until you add sugar or ice cream!

It likes to be in fertile soil and will produce for many years with minimum care. It is hardy to Zone 3, and it will survive in colder zones if mulched. It does like a minimum cool period over the winter with daily temperatures of 5 C (40 F).

Rhubarb does go to seed; however, because these seeds usually don't produce plants similar to their parents, it is recommended to propagate with pieces of root that include buds. These are often called crowns and are available from several outlets, including family and friends.

Keeping in mind that rhubarb can grow more than three feet tall and may spread four to five feet; you should carefully consider where it is to call home. It likes full sun with fertile, well-drained, slightly acidic soil. It is not too crazy about heavy clay or poorly drained areas. Although, having said that, I have seen it grow just about anywhere!

To plant your new vegetable, you will need a hole that is one and a half to two feet deep and approximately two feet in diameter. In the bottom of the hole, place six inches of compost or well-rotted manure. If you do live in an area that has lots of clay, it is recommended to add some coarse sand to the mixture going into the hole. Leaving a depression for the crown, fill the hole with a compost/topsoil mixture. Set the crown into the hole and cover the buds with an inch (2.54 cm) of soil. Water. Planting deeper may cause long spindly stalks. To keep weeds under control and soil moist, mulch with a mixture of compost with straw or shredded leaves mixed in.

Your plant will not disappoint you if you keep the soil moist but not soggy. Harvesting in the first year of planting is not recommended. This will permit the rhubarb to devote all its energies to developing a good root system. The second year, pull only a few stalks. Spread this harvest out over a few weeks to allow the plant to continue growing and not go into shock. The third year, much like the asparagus plant, will be the year to harvest continually. Harvesting more than half the plant at one time may cause production to suffer, and there is a technique to pulling your crop!

Cutting the stalks with a knife or other sharp object leaves open wounds that are susceptible to disease. For best results, grasp the stalk at the bottom and pull upward slightly twisting. With on-going harvesting and regular moisture either from Mother Nature or the garden hose, you should have rhubarb through the fall.

You may enjoy nibbling on the stalks straight from the garden or try one of the various recipes we have collected for you. Be sure to read through the Helpful Hints for more information on what you can do with rhubarb.

Rhubarb can be stored in the fridge for up to two weeks if it is wrapped in a paper towel and sealed in a plastic bag. If freezing your harvest, keep in mind that the texture and flavour will not be quite the same as freshly pulled; however, it will be an added treat during the winter months. To have fresh rhubarb all year, you may want to try forcing rhubarb.

NOTE:
Rhubarb leaves should not be eaten as they contain high amounts of oxalic acid.

Some people who compost do not recommend placing rhubarb leaves in the compost pile. It is thought that the toxicity of the leaf may kill some of the good bugs needed for a successful compost.

ComfyCountryCreations.com

Note from the Author

Fruit or vegetable?

Rhubarb, the much-maligned plant, is continually in the debate limelight each season it appears.

History tells us of the flavourful preserves and baked goods made from its juicy and sometimes tart stalks. The guided tour we are taken on from vintage recipes makes us think of it as a fruit.

The reality is, rhubarb is a vegetable and one that has travelled the world to eventually riddle homesteads across the land. A mainstay for many of the generations that came before us, it is now often the only memory that remains. The huge leaves are found decades and centuries later, in places where people or buildings no longer exist.

It is a vegetable that is hardy in both the coldest of winters and the hottest days of summer. Its tight red nubs push through the still cold soil to flourish throughout the summer, and late into the fall. Modern gardeners often use this vegetable as a filler because of its height and longevity during the growing season. Pulling the stalks to thin them out makes room for more growth and additional harvests.

In the pages of **From Our Home To Yours: Homestead Vegetables-Rhubarb**, this vegetable embarks on yet another journey, this time a culinary one. Travelling from the homestead of long ago into the current century by way of recipes and other interesting ideas shared from family and friends.

We hope you will enjoy making our selection of hand-picked recipes as much as we do. Be sure to record your notes — the next generation will be thankful to have them.

From Our Home To Yours,

Ann Edall-Robson

Books by Ann E. Robson

From Our Home To Yours: Cookies

From Our Home to Yours: Cakes & Squares

Books by Ann Edall-Robson

The Quiet Spirits

Moon Rising: An Eclectic Collection of Words

Birds in my Canadian Backyard

From Our Home To Yours:
Homestead Vegetables - Rhubarb

References

Ann Edall-Robson Cookbook Library
AnnEdallRobson.com
ComfyCountryCreations.com
Eileen Edall Cookbook Library
From Our Home To Yours: Cookies
Lynn Kirkpatrick Cookbook Library

Homestead Vegetables - Rhubarb

www.ingramcontent.com/pod-product-compliance
Lightning Source LLC
Chambersburg PA
CBHW060425010526
44118CB00017B/2362